SUPERSTARS
of
WRESTLING

CHARLOTTE FLAIR

HOT TOPICS

BY BENJAMIN PROUDFIT

 Gareth Stevens
PUBLISHING

Please visit our website, www.garethstevens.com. For a free color catalog of all our high-quality books, call toll free 1-800-542-2595 or fax 1-877-542-2596.

Library of Congress Cataloging-in-Publication Data

Names: Proudfit, Benjamin, author.
Title: Charlotte Flair / Benjamin Proudfit.
Description: New York : Gareth Stevens Publishing, [2019] | Series:
Superstars of Wrestling | Includes index.
Identifiers: LCCN 2017047240| ISBN 9781538220993 (Library bound) | ISBN
9781538221013 (Paperback) | ISBN 9781538221020 (6 pack)
Subjects: LCSH: Flair, Charlotte. | Women wrestlers--United
States--Biography. | Fathers and daughters--United States--Biography.
Classification: LCC GV1196.F59 P76 2019 | DDC 796.812--dc23 LC record available at
https://lccn.loc.gov/2017047240

First Edition

Published in 2019 by
Gareth Stevens Publishing
111 East 14th Street, Suite 349
New York, NY 10003

Designer: Sarah Liddell
Editor: Kristen Nelson

Photo credits: Cover, p. 1 CHRISTOF STACHE/Stringer/AFP/Getty Images; pp. 5, 23
Joachim Sielski/Stringer/Bongarts/Getty Images; pp. 7, 17 TheBellaTwins1445/Wikimedia
Commons; pp. 9, 13, 29 Orlando Sentinel/Contributor/Tribune News Service/Getty
Images; pp. 11, 21 Hopeful Duck/Wikimedia Commons; pp. 15, 25 FlickrWarrior/
Wikimedia Commons; p. 19 Starship.paint/Wikimedia Commons; p. 27 Tabercil/
Wikimedia Commons.

Printed in the United States of America

CPSIA compliance information: Batch #CS18GS: For further information contact Gareth Stevens, New York, New York at 1-800-542-2595.

CONTENTS

THE QUEEN OF WWE

When it comes to high-flying, **athletic** female wrestlers, Charlotte Flair is one of the best in the world! As a Superstar in World Wrestling Entertainment (WWE), Charlotte has accomplished a lot in just a few years in the ring.

IN THE RING

Charlotte's father is Ric Flair, who is in the
WWE Hall of Fame. He's considered by some to
be the best WWE Superstar of all time.

5

BORN AND RAISED

Charlotte was born Ashley Fliehr on April 5, 1986. Her family lived in Charlotte, North Carolina. Charlotte had one younger brother, Reid, and a half brother and half sister, David and Megan. Their dad was often on the road wrestling when they were young.

IN THE RING

Even though she seems to be named after her city,
Charlotte has said she didn't choose her
in-ring name because of that. It was chosen
for her when she started with the WWE.

7

SPORTS STAR

Charlotte has been a **competitive** athlete since childhood. She did gymnastics and cheerleading. At 5 feet 10 inches (1.8 m) tall, she was a great volleyball player. Her high school volleyball team won two state championships. She was named **MVP** and Player of the Year.

IN THE RING

Charlotte has said her sports background helped her pick up wrestling quickly when she started learning in-ring movements.

9

Charlotte was such a good volleyball player that she went on to play volleyball at Appalachian State University in 2005 and 2006. Charlotte then went to North Carolina State University where she finished school, though she didn't play volleyball there.

IN THE RING

After graduating from North Carolina State University, Charlotte became a personal trainer.

THE FAMILY BUSINESS

In 2008, Ric Flair **retired** from WWE wrestling. Charlotte went to WrestleMania 24 that year to see her father's last match. At that point, she wasn't interested in becoming a wrestler herself. Both her brothers were, though!

IN THE RING

Charlotte was on TV as a teenager as part
of some of her dad's wrestling shows!

13

In 2012, Charlotte's father was being entered into the WWE Hall of Fame for a second time. While there, her brother Reid and others at WWE suggested that Charlotte think about signing a contract with the company.

IN THE RING

Charlotte is often asked if she's worried about being in her father's shadow. In 2017, she said "I want to be as memorable as my dad, in my own way, carrying on his **legacy**."

A few months later, Charlotte signed with WWE. She began training with Florida Championship Wrestling (FCW), which became NXT later that year. Though she had never wrestled before, she was already very fit and learned fast.

IN THE RING

Charlotte's younger brother Reid was also trying to make it as a wrestler. He died in 2013, which made Charlotte even more driven to succeed.

17

MAKING IT IN NXT

In July 2013, Charlotte **debuted** on the TV show *NXT*. Her father was there and even introduced her as she headed to the ring. She faced Bayley in her first match—and won! In 2014, she was voted Rookie of the Year by wrestling fans.

TRIPLE H

IN THE RING

At WrestleMania 30 in April 2014, Charlotte was part
of WWE Superstar Triple H's entrance.

Charlotte won her first championship at the NXT TakeOver special event on May 29, 2014. She beat Natalya for the NXT Women's Championship by using her finishing move bow down to the queen.

IN THE RING

Charlotte, along with Becky Lynch, Sasha Banks, and Bayley, began calling themselves the Four Horsewomen in NXT.

SASHA
BANKS

21

WWE DIVA

In July 2015, Charlotte, Becky Lynch, and Sasha Banks were brought up from NXT to be on the main WWE **roster**. All three women began appearing in the Divas, or female wrestlers, **division** on the biggest WWE shows: *Raw* and *SmackDown*.

IN THE RING

Charlotte won the Divas Championship from Nikki Bella in September 2015 at the Night of Champions **pay-per-view** (PPV)!

23

WOMEN'S CHAMP

Charlotte was going into WrestleMania 32 on April 3, 2016, as the Divas Champion. Then, WWE announced the WWE Women's Championship title would take its place. Charlotte was in the match for this new title at WrestleMania—and won!

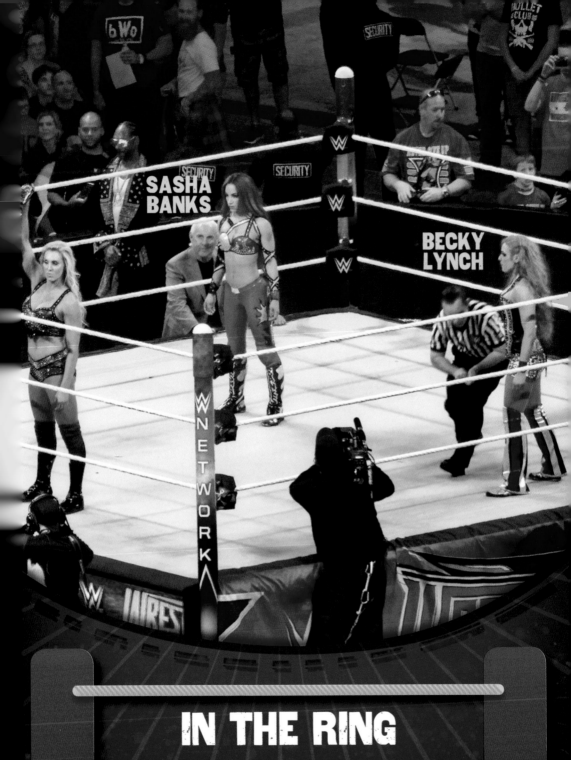

SASHA BANKS

BECKY LYNCH

IN THE RING

Following WrestleMania 32, the WWE Divas started being called Superstars, just like the male wrestlers. Charlotte liked this change!

25

THE MAIN EVENT

In July 2016, WWE split the Superstars for their two main shows. Charlotte went to *Raw*. She became the first holder of the renamed title—the Raw Women's Championship. In October, she and Sasha Banks became the first women to be the main event of a PPV!

IN THE RING

Charlotte won 16 PPV matches in a
row—including the match against Sasha Banks!

27

MANIA!

MANIA!

Charlotte made her mark on
WrestleMania 33 in a Fatal
4-Way match for the Raw
Women's Championship
against Bayley, Sasha Banks,
and Nia Jax. Bayley won, but
Charlotte fights on every week
for another shot at a title!

BAYLEY

IN THE RING

Charlotte started appearing on *SmackDown Live* right after WrestleMania 33.

THE BEST OF
CHARLOTTE

SIGNATURE MOVES

moonsault, powerbomb

FINISHERS

figure-eight leglock, natural selection,
bow down to the queen

ACCOMPLISHMENTS

NXT Women's Champion, WWE Divas
Champion, WWE Women's Champion,
WWE Raw Women's Champion; first
female Superstar to have been in singles
main events on all of *Raw*, *SmackDown*,
and a WWE PPV

MATCH TO WATCH

Charlotte vs. Sasha Banks vs. Becky
Lynch for the WWE Women's
Championship at WrestleMania 32

FOR MORE INFORMATION

BOOKS

Pantaleo, Steve. *How to Be a WWE Superstar*. New York, NY: DK Publishing, 2017.

Scheff, Matt. *Pro Wrestling's Greatest Faces*. Minneapolis, MN: SportsZone, 2017.

WEBSITES

Charlotte Flair
www.wwe.com/superstars/charlotte-flair
Check out Charlotte's official page on the WWE website.

CharlotteFlair.com
charlotteflair.com/
This fan website is updated after Charlotte's every match!

GLOSSARY

athletic: being physically fit and taking part in sporting events

competitive: having to do with an event in which people try to beat others

debut: to appear for the first time

division: a group of people within a larger company

legacy: something that is passed down from someone

MVP: most valuable player

pay-per-view: an event that can only be seen on a TV channel if viewers pay a fee

retire: to leave a job

roster: the list of people who are on a team

INDEX